RELATIONSHIP COMMANDER
Hidden Knowledge of a Happy Relationship

Louis Etu

All rights to this book are reserved. No permission is given for any part of this book to be reproduced, transmitted in any form or means, electronic or mechanical, stored in a retrieval system, photocopied, recorded, scanned, or otherwise. Any of these actions requires the proper written permission of the publisher.

All Rights Reserved

Copyright © 2021

Louis Etu

Disclaimer

All erudition contained in this book is given for informational and educational purposes only. The author is not in any way accountable for any results or outcomes that emanate from using this material. Constructive attempts have been made to provide information that is both accurate and effective, but the author is not bound for the accuracy or use/misuse of this information.

Table of Contents

INTRODUCTION 7
CHAPTER 1 10
   HOW ABOUT A RELATIONSHIP? 10
CHAPTER 2 17
   PURPOSE OF A RELATIONSHIP 17
CHAPTER 3 22
   10 REASONS TO BE IN A RELATIONSHIP 22
CHAPTER 4 26
   TYPES OF RELATIONSHIPS 26
CHAPTER 5 35
   COLORS OF A RELATIONSHIP 35
CHAPTER 6 41
   RELATIONSHIP GOALS 41
CHAPTER 7 49
   THE ART OF COURTING 49
CHAPTER 8 53
   WHY COURTSHIP? 53
CHAPTER 9 57
   PROCESS OF COURTSHIP 57
CHAPTER 10 60

WHAT SHOULD BE DISCUSSED DURING COURTSHIP 60

CHAPTER 11 64
ONSHORE AND OFFSHORE COURTSHIP 64

CHAPTER 12 72
PHILOSOPHY OF MARRIAGE 72

CHAPTER 13 76
PURPOSE OF MARRIAGE 76

CHAPTER 14 80
THE STAGES OF MARRIAGE 80

CHAPTER 15 85
INTIMACY IN MARRIAGE 85

CHAPTER 16 99
PROBLEMS IN MARRIAGE 99

CHAPTER 17 106
MARRIAGE AS A WAY OF LIFE 106

CONCLUSION 109

INTRODUCTION

The discourse of this phenomenon has been widely embraced and explained. Authors, researchers, ministers of God, sociologists, and psychologists have rendered their view, research, and experiences on this topic. It is not surprising that people still have complications in human life because individual makeup is different. What a relationship entails will be discussed in this book while the individual in question applies it to where necessary in their lives: character, perception, and reaction.

This is a progressive discussion of relationship which leads to courtship and eventually, marriage. We will observe that one way or the other, we cherish companionship. We like to have a company of ours, our people, and our circle. This desire to have a companion or companions is embedded in our makeup. A baby needs his mother's company, children want the company of their playmates, and people of like-minds like to retain the people in their circle.

At any point in time, human desires company. The reason for desiring and having companionship differs according to their usefulness to the individuals involved. People start friendship for different reasons; it could be work-related, study-related, ministry partners, and business partners, to mention but a few.

The main focus that will be expounded in this book is companionship and friendship that leads to a relationship. A relationship is a startup for the journey of forever with whoever we choose to be with. The purpose of relationship is also expressed in this book. Brace up for enlightenment as you open the pages of this book.

'Two are better than one, because they have a good reward for their toil. For if they fall, one will lift up his fellow. But woe to him who is alone when he falls and has not another to lift him up! Again, if two lie together, they are warm, but how can one be warm alone? And though a man might prevail against one who is alone, two will withstand him—a threefold cord is not quickly broken.'

~Ecclesiastes 4:9-12 {RSV}

CHAPTER 1

HOW ABOUT A RELATIONSHIP?

'There are friends who pretend to be friends, but there is a friend who sticks closer than a brother'

~Proverbs 18:24{RSV}

The place of friendship is a platonic state where making friends and staying as friends is defined. People move from this platonic stage, having observed attraction between both parties, decides to take the friendship into another state, which is a relationship.

Now, having a relationship with yourself helps you connect with somebody else. In essence being able to love and care for yourself gives you the ability and capacity to care for someone else. How do I have a relationship with myself?

"You cannot give what you don't have."

Being able to be thankful for the gift of life opens up a door of gratitude and looking forward to the things you can control, like:

- Your attitude towards yourself (How you treat yourself)

- Your thoughts about the future

- How honest are you to yourself?

- What you eat (Eating healthy and exercising)

- How often you give time to appreciate nature and life.

Starting from you having a relationship with yourself gives you a free check to know and relate with your partner to be in the new phase you are planning to go into. A relationship is sustained in the existing place of friendship. In friendship, you are not erotically attracted to the opposite sex. Your attraction at first is based on platonic interest and similar things you two have in common. A platform must have connected you two before you come in contact and decide to be friends.

Before you decide or agree with your partner to enter into a relationship with them, some values, inclinations, and orientations must have been similar if not the same with yours. When you observe attraction, closeness, love, commitment in several ways you are beginning to take place in the friendship; you may see the need to define the friendship, if it is still a platonic friendship or moving towards a love relationship.

Considering a relationship requires you to mark out some essential features of the partner you want. You will need to ask yourself specific questions about the individual's character emotional stability, sense of commitment, purpose, service to God and humanity, aspirations, and the future.

In order of importance, it is crucial that the person you want to date is a believer and not just a believer but also rooted in God. Emotional stability and mutual agreement are also important. This is the reason for friendship; friendship will allow you to know if this person is worth being with, or you should forfeit the idea.

If any of your expectations or desire of who you want your partner to be is compromised at all, you should not compromise your basic and acceptable values. You should not compromise your faith. Love is a good factor, but emotions should not overtake the judgment of who and what is good for you.

'The righteous choose their friends carefully, but the way of the wicked leads them astray.'

~Proverbs 12:26{NIV}

Approaching a person with the intent to date or consenting to a relationship requires you to know the kind of person he/she is and if he/she tallies with your prospect. Take your time to make the right decision. Ask God for guidance and be patient to listen.

A lot of people think it is only love that matters, Unwavering love matters to always ignite the chemistry between you two. But it is not the only determinant of who you go into a relationship with. Take into consideration the necessary subjects before you make your decision.

Entering a relationship doesn't mean you can break up, but if the necessary things are considered before entering a relationship, it may reduce the likelihood of breakups, lovers experience. Though there are sometimes circumstances like compatibility or blood group contributes to breakups, but it is essential to thoroughly check in other to avert such.

Furthermore, a relationship is based not only on looks but on the understanding of the individuals and how well they are compatible with each other.

In fact, being in a relationship makes you stronger and less vulnerable. Most people get in a relationship in the first place to fill the void in their hearts and to feel accepted of who they truly are. Some even choose to be in a relationship just to experience it, some are in it for the sake of it while most of them; including you and I are in it for companionship. After all, being alone sucks and we would rather be with someone than a tub of chocolate ice cream, right?

To get to the point where a person feels like they have chosen the right "Partner" they need to start a relationship from zero and build up from there. Everyone has their definition of what relationship means. For some people, it just means knowing someone on the surface; others believe that the real connection is learning all the flaws and positives of the person and loving your partner. When two persons take each other for who they indeed are, when they try to make themselves and each other better for a promising future – this is an authentic, loving relationship.

CHAPTER 2

PURPOSE OF A RELATIONSHIP

'Do two walk together unless they have agreed to do so?'

~Amos 3:3 {NIV}

As we already talked about how to be the right partner and build a healthy relationship with self, now it is time for you to understand why relationship matters and its purpose deeply.

There is always a reason, a motive behind every decision and action. It is unlikely for two or more people to decide what reason or purpose for such a decision to be made. As individuals who have agreed to enter a love relationship, there should be a reason behind your decision. What prompted it? What will be the purpose of your relationship? What fruits will your relationship birth? Are you committed to growing together? How do you plan to enjoy the relationship? These and many other questions are up for an answer.

It should be settled in your mind and partner's mind, the purpose of your relationship. It would help if you discussed what your needs and realistic expectations are. When I say expectation, I don't mean high hopes of building a castle in the air. It simply means discussing in understandable terms what and how the relationship will be built, sustained, and enjoyed by both of you.

Considering the other person's needs and concerns helps you to be selfless and more intimate. Being there for each other when there is no other human to give help or hope is a tie that binds you closer. As you begin to discover more about your partner, you will also know more about yourself because the other person will make you realize it.

Your commitment becomes more substantial when your relationship is purposeful. If you start a relationship without purpose, it is like driving a car without a direction. It is pretty much easy to know the purpose of a relationship if the lovers involved are serious-minded and purposeful being themselves.

Now, the question is, what should the purpose of a relationship be? The answer to the question is relative to the individuals involved, but certain yardsticks can serve as an example of the purpose of a relationship.

A relationship must be premised on honesty, trust, willingness to compromise, sense of completeness of individual, patience, tolerance, understanding, compatibility, communication, and faith. If you don't possess this list or are not good at some, you will realize the need to work on yourself. You won't only see the positive changes being useful for a relationship; it also helps your self-image.

The purpose of a relationship is to get to know each other beyond the peripheral of platonic knowledge, and I am not in any insinuating sexual knowledge. No. it is to set realistic goals for the future, find each other's company to be a place of joy and happiness. Encourage and support each other's aspirations, see the compatibility features, and nurture them, and most importantly, know each other's God-given purpose.

More also the only purpose of a relationship is to love and be loved; it is to live as a complete person because other halves complete us. Having children is fruitful of love. So, love is the initial of every decision we make. A healthy relationship helps us to be in love. Imagine a scenario where the reason for your relationship was something unrestricted and something that you could assume liability for. For example, Rehearsing love — of self as well as other people.

Communication and understanding should be your topmost priority because this will help you to build a purposeful relationship.

CHAPTER 3

10 REASONS TO BE IN A RELATIONSHIP.

"Therefore encourage one another and build each other up, just as in fact you are doing."

~1 Thessalonians 5:11 {NIV}

- Know that it is beneficial for you to be in a relationship. Statistics indicate that married people live longer than their counterparts who are unmarried. They have higher levels of satisfaction, as well. There is no crime in being single-it may be your fate, but marriage does seem to make sense from a health point of view.

- More opportunities, wealth, and fun are also created by those who continue to make more love in their lives. When you have someone by your side who aims for the same goals, it is much easier to reach them.

- To make us better people. We also have the power to do stuff for others that we don't do for ourselves. Love in that way is healthy. He or she is a keeper if your partner brings out the best of you.

- When you have a companion, you will get something done. It's a matter of encouragement sometimes. It's so good to have company sometimes. Four hands will get more done than two, whatever the cause. It's also helpful to bring your heads and hearts together.

- It can be much simpler to turn stuff around than you thought. We are typically either stubborn or resentful. It can help make you more understanding by lowering your attitude and appreciating that your other half has put up with your peccadilloes.

- You are doing your partner something right, "just because," which makes life sweeter for you both. Do nice things for no good cause, and when the favor is returned, be appreciative. Life doesn't offer us many lunches for free.

- Most individuals have more fun playing with others. For some, doing things by yourself can be very rewarding; however, many people prefer the thought of sharing life with a partner.

- . It is validating to have someone who knows you in-depth. It's the gift of understanding that you don't ignore the excellent stuff, and that's why you do so.

- In romance, warmth, hope, and happiness are created. The more you get, the more your life will be fun for you. It sounds easy, and it sounds simple.

- Getting a hand to grab as you go through life makes it easier to manage the challenges we face

When things go wrong, you will be able to go through everything you must and come out on the other side a more optimistic person, trusting that your partner got your back.

CHAPTER 4

TYPES OF RELATIONSHIPS

"Be devoted to one another in love. Honor one another above yourselves."

~Romans 12:10 {NIV}

It is time to analyze and discuss how many types of relationships exist because, trust me, not all of them are healthy or loving. You need to understand what you are looking for, so you do not get trapped into something unpleasing and unwanted.

Among hundreds and hundreds of variations of relationship, society, and the scientists had decided to define five main categories. Sure, not all the relationships strictly fit these categories;

maybe some are between them, perhaps some have elements of two or more of them. However, by defining these five, the most common and known types of relationships, you will get a clearer idea of which one is right and yours. This guide will also help you choose the potent, secure, proper connection over something unhealthy and tragic. In our quest to grasp, control, untangle or command our relationships, we are continually trying to see them through different lenses, failing to link the dots: is it about him or me? Was the tension just a blip over the last few weeks due to stress or the tip of the iceberg of some more significant issues? But it's also important to step back to see the broader landscape to make sense of the union's state better.

Type 1: Controlling & Competitive

- The power of the way better, who wins the debate, whose goals, and criteria we are meeting, and whose work is more important, is jockeying. Many disputes quickly turn into power struggles and fight to get the last word. The emotional climate for this type of relationship is conflict all the time. Underlying dynamics can be seen as two influential personalities competing for control; self-esteem focused on winning, being in charge; frequently rigid ideas about how best to do things, expectations for success, what makes a successful life. In the long term, usually, these couples get tired of fighting and divorce, or one eventually admits, or both finally establish their turfs that they are in control of.

Type 2: Active & Passive

- One partner is mostly responsible for and raises the relationship heavily, while the other partner goes along. While some of these start with a concise competition, this imbalance has been more frequently there since the beginning.

There are few arguments, but the active individual will often feel resentful about bearing the burden or not having enough praise. They blow up or act out but then feel bad and go back to the same role. Climate is usually neutral. Their attitudes are driven by being sweet, making others happy, being over-responsible, avoiding confrontation. They were good kids as teenagers. The more passive partner can be easily overcome by anxiety, feel right or overwhelmed as an adult, and lean on others. In the long term, the active partner gets burned out and leave. The partner left behind either needs to become more independent or find someone else to take over.

Type 3: Aggressive & Accommodating

- The disparity in power here is based not on caretaking but raw power. One partner is obviously in control, and less out of passivity and more out of fear, the other accommodates. Although it can quickly blow up the threatening partner, there is no real conflict. Emotional abuse and often physical abuse are present. Climate is usually high stress; the host partner still walks on eggshells. The bully who has anger-management problems is an aggressive partner. In a home with an abusive parent, he or she might have grown up and learned to identify with that parent. Underneath, there could be high anxiety that translates into intense control, or just a disorder of character that translates to narcissism, power, and little empathy for others. The accommodating partner could have grown up to be victimized and have a greater tolerance for such behavior. Intermittent actions, the other person being sweet sporadically, keeps the partner off balance and fuels magical thinking: I can prevent the other from bursting if I only find out the right steps in the dance. They can never find out the steps, sadly. And in the long term, either the partnership persists, or eventually, the accommodating spouse gets the courage to quit. To drag the other back into the block, the violent partner will do what is required. If that doesn't work, someone else could be identified by the abusive spouse to replace the other one.

Type 4: Disconnected & Parallel Lives

- There is little contention, but little relation as well. With both getting their schedules, they go on autopilot. They have nothing in common; they are more roommates than lovers. The relationship seems stale. Climate is bland, stale, mild stress, and it is usually cold between the two. Usually, within many years, several couples collapse into this form of partnership. It could be that for the wrong reasons they married, what chemistry was there rapidly faded, or from the beginning, they swept problems under the rug and learned to use distance to avoid igniting any dispute. Others may shift into this mellowing relationship that often comes with aging, and still, others become child-centered and have little to keep them together once the kids have left home. Their default subjects of discussion are the weather, work, and updates on children. Overtime crises in midlife or older age may cause one or both to feel that time is running out. This can precipitate arguing and attempts to either ultimately revitalize or exit the relationship. Or they keep telling themselves it's good enough, or they're too old to move on.

Type 5: Accepting & Balanced

- The couple can work as a team together, complementing each other. They each consider the strengths of the other and consciously embrace them. They have the back of each other; both are involved in having the other be who he or she would like to be. When it starts to grow old, they can revitalize the relationship; they can fix problems instead of brushing them under the rug. Climate: Loving, calm, although som-

stressful periods of change may occur. Dynamics: They may start this way, or they may have begun with either of the other types but have managed to make things better through counseling or wisdom and resolve. Long-term: Crises in midlife and older age can occur, but they will work through them. We're drawing a gloomy picture of the first four, clearly, but basically, it's not 24/7 grimness. There are either only enough positive interactions to prevent the relationship from going under entirely, or children's obligations include much emphasis or diversion to sustain a long-term partnership. Accepting and balanced relationship is the one everybody strives for. This one follows through what the bible teaches us: Colossians 3:14: "And over all these virtues put on love, which binds them all together in perfect unity."

A committed relationship involves two people who have decided to walk together in love, esteem the other above his/her and count the other person as a significant part of their lives. They share opinions, values and aspirations, care, concern, and purpose. The relationship is predicated on godly virtues. It is this sort of relationship that has hope for the future.

Choose and choose wisely. Peer influence doesn't do anyone well; neither does been led by emotion secure a healthy relationship. As sweet as being in a relationship is, ensure you take your time to make the right choice for yourself.

CHAPTER 5

COLORS OF A RELATIONSHIP

"There is no fear in love, but perfect love drives out fear, because fear has to do with punishment, the one who fears is not made perfect in love"

~1 John 4:18 {NIV}

There are so many colors of a relationship and every color resembles a rainbow because of the different emotions. From red to indigo, we go through all kinds of sentiment and passion that often works with or against us. Let's dig a little deeper into what each color associates.

1 – **Red:** As we all know, red is the color of love, but did you know that red can also be the color of anger? Yes, red may not always be all lovey-

dovey as couples may fight or get into silly arguments, but the most important reason love is red is because a fight can ignite a strange passion between you and your partner. A fight can bring you both closer and can help you understand each other better. Perhaps that may be the reason why red represents love and anger.

2 - **Orange:** Orange is associated with playfulness and pleasure. If you and your partner have a good relationship, then its most likely that you both will have moments where you will joke and laugh around. It's a good thing to think of your partner as your best friend because that way, your relationship will feel less of a burden and you will also be open about your emotions to them.

3 - **Yellow:** When we think of yellow, we think of happiness because yellow is something that makes us happy and feel joy. Have you ever felt pure bliss whenever you looked at your partner?

It's like your heart will burst and everything around will just turn glittery as if you're in a Unicorn world. I have felt that way sometimes and I'm sure many of you have as well. When your significant other makes you happy, it's a sign of true love and it shows how loyal and caring they are to you.

4. Green: Have you ever felt envy whenever your partner would look at someone else even though you know that they are just glancing out of curiosity? Or when your partner says that he/she loves so-and-so actor or actress? Well, that's a sure sign that you're going all green! your jealousy is getting the best of you and it's time you check your feelings again because sometimes, going green isn't going to work with your partner. To be a happy and life-long couple, you need to trust each other and keep aside all those jealous feelings. Sure, there is a good envy and bad envy but make sure to realize which side of it you're leaning most to.

5. Blue: Ever heard of the feeling, 'I'm feeling blue?' that's because blue is associated with sadness. A relationship isn't perfect without shedding tears. You may shed them when you're angry, sad, or happy but tears also bring you closer to each other because it shows how vulnerable you are and that you're in need of some protection and consolation. But ladies, that doesn't mean you will cry every other day! Keep your tears in limits and know that no matter how blue you feel, your partner will always rush to your aid with a box of tissues.

6. Indigo: When you look at the color Indigo, what do you feel? Tranquility and calmness, right? That's what you feel when you look at your soul mate. Your anxieties fade away and you suddenly feel stronger than ever. For me, when I look at my spouse I feel as though I am floating in space and everything around me is just filled with happiness. All my worries seem to run away, and I feel more motivated and productive to do my daily chores and activities. Love really does give you energy!

7. Violet: Violet represents endless love. A relationship becomes much sweeter if there's constant attraction and skinship because without it, the bond between you and your partner may dither and wither. Violet not only brings joy but satisfaction as well and I think we can all agree that every relationship needs a bit of a violet to keep them going.

The secret to having a perfect relationship is to have all the colors of the rainbow in perfect balance and harmony. Even if one of them has too much and the other has less, then it's more likely that your relationship may not be going in the right path. However, everyone has their own way of dealing with relationships and if you believe that you must keep one color your priority and the other secondary, then go ahead and bloom that flower of love!

But my advice would be—just like you eat colorful vegetables—give your partner a rainbow of emotions as well. It will keep your relationship strong and healthy.

CHAPTER 6

RELATIONSHIP GOALS

"Be completely humble and gentle; be patient, bearing with one another in love."

- Ephesians 4:2 {NIV}

A relationship needs communication to achieve growth. In fact, the more you communicate with your partner, the longer your relationship will last. Sometimes, you can compromise but it isn't always an available option and there is the tendency for you to feel like you're losing your freedom.

You can't keep pretending as though you are happy in a relationship because it will eventually show sooner or later. The only thing you can do is to sit down and proffer solutions to any problems that may come your way. However, such problems can be avoided in part or on both whole by establishing relationship goals that will not prevent you from just arguments and heartaches alone but also from unpleasant surprises. Both of you can also plan and achieve your set goals together. This will help make your relationship grow stronger.

With the relationship goals that follow, I can assure you that you can enhance the relationship between you and your partner. In achieving these goals, you will learn more about the values of your partner and both of you will have something to look forward to in the future.

Goal #1 - Prioritize Each Other

As we make progress on our individual goals, there is a tendency to get distant from our respective partners. This is because our focus starts tilting to our individual materialistic goals rather than our future goals as a couple. We tend to neglect the needs and desires that our partner has and gradually lose connection with them.

However, if you can learn to manage your own goals while fulfilling your partner's needs at the same time, you can achieve a win-win situation for you. You'll feel happier and content with your life.

There's no doubt that your relationship should be your priority regardless of anything else because of the input to build trust, integrity, and communication that you have put into the relationship.

One thing both of you can do is to sit down and commit to each other every morning before you go to work or every night after the day's work. Show your partner love. Give them your time. Speak with them and understand their feelings. While this may seem like an easy task, not many people have been able to achieve it. It requires continuous recalibration because both of you live different lives even though you're connected.

This is why both of you have to come to the realization and acceptance that your partner is like your life source. You then work on how to give them time. But remember to give time for your future progress too. There's no easy way to do this but if you're consistent with it, then you and your partner will definitely love to be around each other more often and you will find yourselves discussing matters that you initially thought wouldn't have been possible. After all, every girl wishes to have someone that would understand her and help her fulfill her dreams and goals.

Goal #2 - Plan Fun Activities Together

Wasn't that feeling amazing when you and your partner were at the stage of dating? When you recall those memories, all the fun times you both had will flood your mind. However, as time passed, your days became hectic and uncontrollable and you both grew apart from each other and all the fun times you both had just disappeared into thin air.

Well, don't be scared because it's not too late to bring those good times back in your life. Both of you can create a schedule you can consider possible that will cater for fun activities that the both of you can enjoy. Trying out new activities together should also do the trick. The goal is for the both of you to spend as much time as possible together so that neither of you will feel left out.

Try bringing back that lost sparkle into your hearts and if you seem to get bored of some activities, go ahead and ditch them. You can try something new and different instead. It's crucial to always make time for your partner even when they utter phrases like, 'it's okay,' or 'don't worry about me.'

Once you learn to prioritize their feelings, you'll start to understand their longing for you. Your relationship can also get to a level where nothing can cause both of you to break apart from each other.

Goal #3 Go to Monthly Movies or Picnic

Considering that neither of you may have time to go to the movies or for a picnic every other week, it's advisable to promise one another (and to keep that promise) to plan towards a monthly movie or picnic at a location of your partner's choosing. You can take turns choosing the movie or the location but that doesn't matter as much.

The point here is for both of you to have fun together and enjoy each other's company. In case you're struggling financially or maybe you hate traveling and are more of a 'stay at home' kind of person, you can hold your picnic in your backyard and maybe in the living room as you watch your chosen movie. There are several ways through which you can spend time together. It's important for both of you to get away from work just gaze into each other's eyes because, in the end, work will not stay with you forever. Your partner will, so learn to acknowledge their presence.

Goal #4 Hug Each Other Often

Hugs make you feel comfortable, secure and they increase your level of intimacy both emotionally and physically. Based on this, you should hug your partner every day just to let them know that you love them. It's a kind of non-verbal communication that works great if you're one that's not too expressive with words or you may be just too shy to say those three magic words.

Goal #5 Have Inside Jokes

Just the way everyone feels jealous when you and one of your siblings laugh at a joke that no one else understands, it's good to have inside jokes with your partner. This helps to increase the intimacy and closeness between the both of you. I love a good inside joke and I'm sure you will too so that you and your partner can crack up whenever any of you is in a bad mood.

CHAPTER 7

THE ART OF COURTING

"Then he went down and talked with the woman, and he liked her"

~Judges14:7 {NIV}

Courtship is the gradual, systemic method of pursuing the other individual in a relationship. It is the romantic way to speak to a person before deciding to accept him or her. It's the idea to become close friends with a person before you become intimate lovers.

Love is a strong word that should be used only when we really mean it. You should not say it just for the sake of saying it the way it is commonly and frivolously used nowadays. Love binds us together and when we act or profess it, it makes the bond stronger. When you are going through the relationship phase and you intend to build a strong one, you might see the necessity of starting or accepting a courtship.

Starting this new phase means that the both of you have seen the qualities you want in each other as a wife/husband and you are convinced that both of you can walk through forever, together.

Courtship is defined as a period during which a couple develops a romantic relationship before they eventually get married. Oftentimes in religious settings, the romantic aspect is left out when discussing courtship, or better put, it is usually not extensively discussed. And this shouldn't be. Emphasizing the don'ts of courtship for the fear of indulging in premarital sex does not tell the whole truth that needs to be learned.

Honestly, you cannot know all about your spouse, but at the same time, there are several things that you will discover during your relationship and courtship. These things will give you insight into who they really are and what exactly it is that they stand for.

The aspect of learning more about your partner before marriage continues and it is the core of courtship. The only difference here is that marriage is envisioned in courtship. Courting should be viewed as a means to an end and the end, in this case, the end is marriage. Once you have marriage in view, you may start to involve your religious leaders and families.

As much as courtship is referred to as a romantic relationship, sex is not encouraged. This is because both of you are not legally, and in biblically ordination, married to each other.

Take time to groom and prepare yourself for marriage. Learn all the necessary things. Hold on to your values, and give room for selflessness. During courtship, you can answer for yourself only if you are mentally, physically, emotionally, financially, and spiritually prepared for marriage.

Equip yourself with sufficient knowledge and be prepared to act on what you've learned. Don't wait until you are about to get married before you start learning about what to do and how to handle certain situations.

CHAPTER 8

WHY COURTSHIP?

"Beloved, let us love and seek the best for one another, for love is from God; and everyone who loves is born of God and knows God."

~1 John 4:7 {AMP}

Marriages were moderately associated with business transactions not too long ago. We tend to forget too often that marriage and the romanticism of relationships is a relatively new phenomenon that is still being worked on by humans. With each passing decade, our society tends to alter the mores of relationship etiquette and as a result, the rate of courtships has decreased.

However, courtship offers a charming chance for both of you to connect and get to know each other. At the courtship stage, both of you develop a closer look at each other, particularly in line with marriage. Objectively, you get to learn and hear about each other. While this stage may overwhelm most young men and women, they can profit from it as they get to know each other's lifestyle at every location. It should be a period when the parties to a partnership should accept sound inquiry into the private and public aspects of their lives.

Courtship brings about the most profound and vital decisions that can be made about the future and life of a partnership and marriage future and life. Many individuals have found out nasty things about their partners. Things they should have missed because of the sense of attraction that might have overcome them. Young people should also use courtship as an opportunity to observe the character of their partners, to test their backgrounds, and discover each other's views.

For some, courtship can be an awkward idea synonymous with terms such as "old-fashioned" and "antiquated." When we hear the word, some of us may think of how it was used in the past as a means for parents to supervise the process of uniting their kids.

Nowadays, many people start their relationships based on superficial intimacy, which is basically just privacy that uses only the pleasant aspects of a normal relationship. Aspects like living with someone, sharing a bed, and having a sexual relationship, all are fun. It's dedication without dedication. The issue with this, especially when kids come into the mix, is that it's still involvement. Couples often tend to realize too late that they are not compatible and this can cause them to end up resenting each other, but there are still the benefits of commitment.

Couples like this may end up with homes that are damaged. Single mothers and fathers end up suffering financially and mentally as they try to make sense of what may have gone wrong. Or worse, without a blueprint for a safe, happy relationship, they raise several kids and the cycle may be repeated.

CHAPTER 9

PROCESS OF COURTSHIP

"Love and faithfulness meet together; righteousness and peace kiss each other."

~Psalm 85:10 {NIV}

Some people may say that it is all "talk" with a person until it's exclusive. However, the difference is that courtship depends on more than just dating factors. Courtship filters attraction to be synchronized with the worldview, personality, and trajectory of someone's life. How does it look like proper courtesy?

This is usually what the process involves: first, you move forward with dates. Get to know the other person by taking them for dinner or to the movies but avoid getting into an exclusive relationship hastily. The best way to do this is to have group dates so that you avoid any confusion. As often as you can, aim to make dates with various kinds of people.

Widen your horizons across various types of personalities. This way you can know more about what kind of person you want to be. The courtships start when you have met someone you're appealing for in the simplest surface way. Ensure that they are aware that before you start anything, you'd like to take things gradually and get to know them first. Regardless of your gender, this is a healthy way to weed out people who don't match up your priorities and beliefs. You should never invest your time or emotional commitment in them if you decide that it isn't valuable to you.

Sooner or later, you will meet someone who is genuinely eager to be courted. Perhaps, they have encountered rushed commitments in the past. Explore who they are and allow them to explore you while courting others. You should have hours of conversation to start during this period. Go for runs, have coffee, hang out, or do whatever you want to do. Doing these without building a bond around it provides an atmosphere where the two of you can be more open about who you are and what you are looking for. Yeah, you're always trying to impress them. So it helps when you court someone and spend time with them because it becomes more challenging for you to hide your true self. And the same thing applies to them. Any elements of courtship can be practiced without you understanding them. You can let the other person know that you care about these things, and you should do this before beginning a deep relationship. Be frank, however. Are you asking the hard questions and getting to know someone?

CHAPTER 10

WHAT SHOULD BE DISCUSSED DURING COURTSHIP

"Submit to one another out of reverence for Christ."

~Ephesians 5:21 {NIV}

Courtship is the time to ask questions that, unless asked correctly, may seem to be a little taboo. Ask your partner what their goals are for important decisions that they will ultimately make. This entails where they want to live, if they wish to be married or not, whether they see themselves settling down, all about children, their jobs, etc. It might seem a little strange to bring these things up now, but you are trying to avoid a relationship with someone who is not compatible with you. On the other hand, if they are, then you can start an exclusive relationship with the person you're drawn to since they are heading in the same direction as you are. Who's not going to want that? Sure, without courtship, you can have a happy relationship. That isn't impossible. However, you should understand that you are rolling the dice on something that you should take very seriously, as it can affect your whole life.

Discussing certain things with your partner can be significant during courtship. Do not be shy to articulate your plans whether they are future or financial goals, aspects of your relationship, and values. Let's look at some of the things that you can discuss with your significant other to-be.

You can start your discussion with finances. Discuss with each other how much you both plan to contribute, how you plan to save, and any other financial responsibilities that may exist. It's alright if you do not go into much detail but these are just some beginner points you can work with and then build-up from there accordingly.

It's better to focus on the relationship prospect more in courtship than at the beginning of your marriage. At the beginning of your marriage, you and your partner will be focused on growing overtime together and making your marriage work. You can ask each other about your roles, how much your in-laws and theirs will be involved, how you both plan to resolve any difference of opinions, and how to divide household responsibilities. Nowadays, the word 'homemaker' doesn't belong to just women but men as well so make sure (especially men) that you don't hastily assume that your to-be partner will stay at home and take care of the household and kids without consulting them.

One more topic you should discuss thoroughly is about kids. How many would you both like to have? Who will take on the role of disciplining them? What would be your roles regarding the studies of your kids? It will be a long and hard topic but remember, you're just discussing things out so fighting over aspects you disagree over isn't going to do the job. Just remain calm and go over each other's points. Ask your partner if they're open to changes and work correspondingly.

Some other topics for you to focus on would be basic values such as loyalty, mutual support, love, mutual respect, commitment, and communication. You can ask yourselves questions about physical intimacy if you want. You can ask about the kind of vacations you both would like, and if needed, if there will be a considerable break between you two? How do you both plan to resolve conflicts and are there any cultural differences you should know about beforehand?

Knowing these simple but significant answers can be vital in saving your marriage.

CHAPTER 11

ONSHORE AND OFFSHORE COURTSHIP

"Since you are precious and honored in my sight, and because I love you, I will give people in exchange for you, nations in exchange for your life."

~Isaiah 43:4 {NIV}

At times, a (long) distance courtship may seem quite uncertain but it sure has its advantages. A (long) distance courtship may evoke unique challenges but on the bright side, you and your partner are going to experience something foreign which most of us are unable to feel. A (long) distance courtship also allows you both to get to know each other without being forced to implement skinship.

I'm not saying that (long) distance courtship is easy. All I'm just saying is that you should not give up because your relationship can work out in ways you didn't even imagine if you and your partner really got to know each other. And if it's God's planning, then not even the seas can stop you from meeting each other someday.

A (long) distance courtship needs you to put in extra work, extra focus, and extra energy to take that next big step in your life. However, it doesn't matter whether you're in Germany and your partner is in California, your job is to stay honest and true to yourself. Telling lies about something can jeopardize your relationship and may have consequences later in the future. (Well, if you're a good liar and can hold onto a lie for so long, then that's a different thing) but I--or anyone in this world would never recommend lying about anything if claim to be serious about your courtship and you want to spend the rest of your life with that person.

As it is written in Ephesians 4:25{NIV} *'Therefore each of you must put off falsehood and speak truthfully to your neighbor (partner), for we are all members of one body'* You should always be transparent about anything you're doing and let your partner know your thoughts, discomfort, and any other problems that you might be having because honestly, honesty is the foundation of all relationships.

Whenever you eventually decide to meet face to face, maximize your time to get to know each other better and make the most of your time together. It's crucial that you reveal your qualities to your partner beforehand so that they can make their decision before it gets too late. Spend time with your in-laws too and avoid being petty and impetuous in making your decisions.

Indeed, hastiness is the devil's work so choose your options wisely. If your long-distance courtship is a successful one, then it will be a story you both will most likely cherish and spread to your children and even your grandchildren.

Making your courtship interesting...

Now, you're at a stage where there's still time before the wedding and you're still getting to know your partner. It's time to make your courtship period slightly more interesting and not boring so that you can have a box full of polaroids that have captured your memories.

This period of courtship can make you realize why you fell in love with your partner in the first place. Spicing things up a little bit will not harm you. Just ensure that you do the things that you and your partner are comfortable with and let everything else play out on their own.

The first thing you want to do is to spend time together more often. Sure, you might be busy but just catching up for several minutes can be very beneficial to both of you. Show your partner that you have time for them even if it's just for an hour a day.

Furthermore, try to be more open with your partner. You must be willing to come out and be your true self. This way they can also experience the same things that you have felt. Both of you are going to be together anyway so why not get slightly romantic and make each other's hearts flutter.

I would also like to point out that this period of courtship is like the golden hour. The better the impression you make on your in-laws, the better things would be for you and your partner. Let them know your traits and don't be afraid to show them your flaws as well. Nobody's perfect!

To make your courtship more interesting, get more involved in planning your wedding. This way, you can even layout breadcrumbs helping your partner know what your likes and dislikes are. This will also be an excellent opportunity for both of you to go on dates and explore new places and experiences on the side.

Ensure you compliment your partner whenever you get the chance to because a compliment can go along way in making their day. Oftentimes, we put focus more on how we look in order to impress our partner. At the end of the day, it's good to acknowledge the hard work they have put into dressing and styling up just for you.

During your courtship, you may discuss your honeymoon. It's not awkward, don't think it is. Just plan out your honeymoon as if both of you are going on a vacation. Trust me, when you get married, all that shyness will likely go away. Having this discussion will also give your partner a sense of relief as it shows your eagerness to be alone with them.

Sometimes, flirting the right way with the right emotions can do the trick too but you do not want to go too far. Know what your partner is like and whether he/she likes to be flirted with or not. If they don't like to be flirted with, then sending cheesy lines in the middle of the night might just annoy them. It's better for you to know their personality before rolling the dice. Pro-tip to the guys: every girl loves a kiss on the cheek.

While men are generally more successful in making their lady's heart flutter by means of sending them heart emojis, women have a special and creative way of making the men's stomach turn and this is through surprises. Women are good at cooking meals and making amazing art. Why not utilize that creativity and send your partner a gift out of pure love? I'm sure he will love it regardless of what it is. Making our courtship interesting will erase any awkwardness between you and your partner. It will also help you flow into the stage of marriage smoothly and without any apprehensions.

CHAPTER 12

PHILOSOPHY OF MARRIAGE

"Therefore, what God has joined together, let no one separate"

~Mark 10:9 {NIV}

"Submitting yourselves one to another in the fear of God. Wives submit yourselves unto your own husbands, as unto the Lord. For the husband is the head of the wife, even as Christ is the head of the church: and he is the savior of the body. Therefore, as the church is subject unto Christ, so let the wives be to their own husbands in everything. Husbands love your wives, even as Christ also loved the church, and gave himself for it; That he might sanctify and cleanse it with the washing of water by the word, that he might present it to himself a glorious church, not having spot, or wrinkle, or any such thing; but that it should be holy and without blemish. So, ought men to love their wives as their own bodies. He that loveth his wife loveth himself. For no man ever yet hated his own flesh; but nourished and cherished it, even as the Lord the church: For we are members of his body, of his flesh, and of his bones. For this cause shall a man leave his father and mother, and shall be joined unto his wife, and they two shall be one flesh. This is a great mystery: but I speak concerning Christ and the church. Nevertheless, let every one of you in particular so love his wife even as himself; and the wife see that she reverences her husband." Ephesians 5:21-33{KJV} This scripture deals with marriage though the entire passage parallels the relationship between Christ and the Church. We can see from these verses that marriage is far more than we expect. For any married couple or anyone wishing to get married, it is necessary to have a profound understanding of God's intent for marriage. It will be impossible for any married couple to fully comprehend the essence or depth of commitment God requires in a marriage without having an awareness of God's meaning. I can't overstate the importance of this. When we advance in life and in marriage, challenges and problems are bound to arise. In coping with these challenges and problems, a profound acceptance and appreciation of God's marriage theory are essential elements around which a Christian marriage revolves around. If a person has the wrong premise, they will skip the why, and sometimes the how of their marriage's existence. Love is supposed to be a lot more than just the physical union of two individuals. It is a relationship that is deeply spiritual and sacred. "A marriage is divinely chosen by God to represent, in human terms, our relationship with God in Salvation" (Greg S. Baker).

Love the one you choose to love. God wants you to choose one person, just one person, to love so unconditionally that you begin to understand God's own love for yourself as you experience the joys and pains of your relationship. It is only then that you can comprehend the pleasure of God when there is reconciliation, His anger when you sin, His jealousy for our time and love, and His joy when a sinner makes restitution within marriage and family. This is God's primary reason for being against divorce. No matter what we do, God will not abandon or forsake us. The only way to understand this is to choose someone you are willing to do the same for. Divorce, therefore, is a rejection of the promise of God to us as well. Choosing to get a divorce suggests that you do not understand the scope of God's devotion to you. It is a rejection of the promises God made out of His love. It means, in a way, that you believe that God may and will divorce you.

CHAPTER 13

PURPOSE OF MARRIAGE

'And the Lord God said, it is not good that the man should be alone; I will make him a help meet for him'

~Genesis 2:18 {KJV}

Marriage is a phenomenon ordained by God. It is the union of a couple in holy matrimony which is to last for as long as the couple is alive. The Bible says the marriage bed should remain undefiled. And the Bible also gives clear instructions on how the couple should accept and view each other.

Many people go into marriage without adequate preparation or a forehand knowledge of who their partner is. This is where relationship and courtship come in. Getting engaged and looking forward together forever is a happy feeling. You get this awesome feeling that you are finally going to marry the partner of your dreams –the euphoria of love and acceptance.

Now, you seem prepared to walk down the aisle. Have you given the idea of living together forever purposefully a deep thought? Have you thought and asked yourself what are your reasons for loving this person and wanting to stay forever in a union with him/her? Do you have common grounds that can hold your decision to remain in the union even when things don't go smoothly or as planned?

Marriage is a longtime commitment and it is an enduring act of selflessness. For you to consciously get to this stage, you must have been equipped with all marriage is about. There are obvious and significant purposes of marriage, which I will be explaining briefly:

To Mirror God's Love and Typify Christ: The Bible commands the husband to love his wife as Christ loves the Church and gave himself for her. Christ is the husband of the Church and he gave His life for His bride. Regardless of what happens, Christ cannot divorce His bride. The Bible says God hates divorce. Essentially, this is saying that marriage shows an aspect of God in man. And this is one reason why God created marriage.

Companionship: Amos 3:3 says "can two walk together unless they agree?" Man needs company. The woman also needs company. Both need to have a companion so that they can both harness their strengths and walk together in love.

Oneness: One of the reasons God created marriage was for oneness. The Bible says in Genesis 2:24 that "the man shall leave his parents and cleave to his wife in a union." They are to become one and God recognizes their oneness.

Fruitfulness: God instructed the man to be fruitful and multiply. Under a union, a marriage union, a couple can become productive and have their own children in line with God's word. God wants His children to be nurtured under the family tree. This is the more reason why the Church and the society need to preach the right perception about family.

To Fulfill God-Ordained Purpose: Each couple has an individual God-given purpose on earth and the coming together of any couple should foster the fulfillment of this purpose.

Check through and digest the purpose of marriage. Examine if you have similar reasons for wanting to enter a marriage covenant. Set your mind on having a purposeful marriage and work things out accordingly.

CHAPTER 14

THE STAGES OF MARRIAGE

"If I have the gift of prophecy and can fathom all mysteries and all knowledge, and if I have a faith that can move mountains, but do not have love, I am nothing."

~1 Corinthians 13:2 {NIV}

Let me clarify one thing -courtship is different from marriage. While marriage is a more intimate affair, courtship can be regarded as 'dating' someone for a period. Marriage is the start of a new family and just like any novel or scientific research, it has its stages. There are a total of five stages in marriage, namely: the romance stage, the adjusting stage, the struggle stage, the friendship stage, and lastly the commitment stage. Beloved, don't get overwhelmed as I will briefly point out what each of these stages means.

Stage 1: Romance Stage. In this stage, you feel as though you're in seventh heaven. Your life seems to turn into a Hollywood romance movie and all you can think of and dream of is your spouse. I, particularly, love this stage because this stage makes you feel like a princess and your spouse is your knight in shining armor. Definitely, women tend to exaggerate a lot in this stage but that's just how this stage works.

Stage 2: Adjusting Stage. This part gets a teeny-tiny bit tricky. This is because in this stage you're on your way to learning a bit more about your spouse. However, your goal is to communicate with them. Tell them about your feelings and thoughts and any concerns you may have about them and resolve any conflicts that both of you may have stumbled upon.

Stage 3: The Struggle Stage: In this stage, couples tend to debate on options such as getting a divorce or not. In this stage, you and your partner will begin to notice each other's faults and differences and would wonder how on earth you fell in love with them. Don't worry, this is a totally natural stage and for some couples, this stage might never even take place. But in case it does, what you need to do is take the first step of recalling why you fell in love with them at first and find at least one good reason why you still love them. As we mature, we tend to change so one can't blame others or take the blame for the changes either. It's up to you to accept fate as it is and to know that what God has planned for you is the right thing for you. Just remember that divorce is not the answer. It never is.

Stage 4: The Friendship Stage: I like this stage a lot because, in this stage, you are required to put your differences, values, beliefs, and most importantly, your ego aside and reconcile with your partner. You become the best friends both of you have always been at the time of courtship. The transition that you experience in this stage is so beautiful that you will be thankful to God every single day for giving you a spouse like no other.

Stage 5: The Commitment Stage: Lastly, this is the stage where you can seal the deal with a kiss because you've successfully passed all the obstacles in your life and you are now stronger together than ever. At this point, no one can break you or pull you apart because both of you are committed to each other now and no one else. This stage is where you can high-five your spouse and kiss your trophy of a perfect relationship.

No two couples are the same. Some take more time to adjust and commit while others are quick on discovering the right judgment of God and moving forward with His plans without any hesitation. Albeit, in the end, your goal is to be together forever and that's what you should aim for as well. Indeed, God has created a soul mate for every soul and you will find yours when the time is right. Just trust in His timing and everything will go well.

CHAPTER 15

INTIMACY IN MARRIAGE

"Let her be as the loving hind and pleasant roe; let her breasts satisfy thee at all times; and be thou ravished always with her love"

~Proverbs 5:19 {KJV}

One thing I love the most about marriages is the sweet, memorable, and vulnerable moments that mean more than anything else in this world to the couple. Even the slightest touch of your spouse's hand on your skin or them greeting you 'good morning' with a smile changes everything and makes you feel on top of the world. And if you truly love that person, that feeling could go on till your last breath.

Like almost any other thing, there are disadvantages of a marriage, for example, your relationship with your in-laws, the constant need for companionship even though your spouse may be busy, and the increase in responsibilities. All these make it hard for a marriage to work properly. This situation can be likened to a clock whose gears have stopped working. However, to make the gears work, you have to oil them. You must not let the clock stop or else you won't realize how much time has passed. Doing all these may seem burdensome but once you grow to love your marriage and every characteristic of your spouse, you will easily live a happy life that most people would be envious of.

Let me clarify one thing. Despite the fact that I have said some very beautiful things, not every marriage is perfect, and not every moment would be a fairy tale. There will be arguments, misunderstandings, sadness and even the urge t:

break the marriage off and run away. But the more patient you are, the more you will learn and understand how marriage works, the more you will understand each other's thoughts and feelings, and comprehend what you can do to make your relationship better and long-lasting.

This advice is not for women only but men as well. Both genders need to, if possible, compromise and adjust in some matters. You should be encouraging your spouse, be the ray of sunshine to them when they're feeling low, and be a teddy bear when they're not in the mood to cook breakfast or dinner for you. You must also learn to focus on each other's strengths and set aside your weaknesses. Try to enjoy everything in your life. Have fun together and don't be strict. Act the way a boyfriend and girlfriend would or better yet, think of your spouse as your best friend and treat them that way.

Every relationship needs a little laughter and kindness. So even if you're going through a tough time, smile a little or share a meal. These acts would seem beneficial not for just the heart but the soul as well.

Marriage is also all about appreciation. You must learn to appreciate each other and the work and effort both of you put into keeping each other happy. Sometimes accepting their critics and making changes for them would strengthen your bond. However, you need to know your limits and when to back out if you feel that doing any of those things is hard for you. Talk it all out with your spouse and let them know your thoughts and feelings; your fears, likes, and dislikes, talk to them more and more, and tell them about yourself. If you don't tell them about yourself, then who will? How will they know what makes you happy and what doesn't?

Treat your marriage like it's a precious and rare gem that you have found. You will realize sooner or later that you will start liking the things you once thought you hated, things about your spouse that you once thought were weird. Marriage is an ambitious and curious path that will make you feel important and loved. There is some truth to marriage in the movies, and God said so Himself in Genesis 2:24, 'Therefore a man shall leave his father and his mother and hold fast to his wife, and they shall become one flesh.'

God has planned a mate for every soul and no matter how long it takes, that soul will find its way to you. That's God's planning after all. It's all about praying and hoping to have a spouse that will love and cherish you and be there for you when all the doors seem to be closed or when you feel like the ocean has dried up. Sacrifices will be made but those sacrifices are what will bring both of you closer to each other. Your spouse will be your shield and sword and they will be your guardian angel who will look after you. So, treat them well. Be good to them and love them the way you have loved no one before.

Here are some tips on how you can have a more satisfying and intimate relationship with your spouse:

Tip 1. Firstly, try finding time to spend with each other instead of running away from conversations that could have happened if you didn't continually have dinner dates with your bosses and clients. You can spend time together by going for a walk at night, dining together, maybe going to a cinema, going shopping or if you are a child at heart, go to an arcade and compete. These small pastimes will play a big role in your life. Take this chance to know more about your spouse. And at the end of the day, appreciate the time they have given you.

Tip 2. Now, I don't want to make this awkward, but this tip is more useful than the previous tip. This tip is physical closeness. It can either be holding hands, sitting together or even simple eye-contact (just ask your spouse to challenge you to a 'Don't Blink' game). Take your time to build up that skinship and when the time comes, you know what's going to happen, so be prepared for that. Okay, sorry, I made this awkward. Let's head on to the third tip.

Tip 3. Sympathize with each other. You need to be open and understanding about each other. You need to let out your feelings to them. It may seem hard initially but once you let the water run, the burden on your shoulders will gradually lighten as your spouse will understand whatever you may be going through. They may even help you overcome it. It's good to just sit together and have a talk that no one, except the stars and the moon, knows about. Perhaps you may realize that your spouse may have been waiting for such a day so that they can be open about their feelings too. So why not roll the dice first and think about the results later?

Tip 4. Ask them what they need help with. Oftentimes, we just assume that our spouse doesn't need any help. It may be that sometimes we are the ones who are too shy to ask for help. But those words, 'how can I help?' are so soothing to the nerves that you immediately feel like sharing the burden with your spouse. Sharing each other's emotions or work will draw both of you closer and you can use this chance to have that conversation you've always wanted to have.

Tip 5. While it's important to be together, it's also important to stay apart. Both of you need to give yourself the 'me' time so that you have th chance to regroup and think things through from a fresh and different perspective. At the end of it all, you can focus on your spouse more and be their cheerleader. Always remember that no matter how big or small the problem may be, sharing it with your partner makes it a lot easier for you to overcome it. You're, after all, in it together.

Tip 6. Never --and I repeat-- never do anything out of spite or vengeance because it will only backfire and the relationship you spent so hard building on might wobble. You must also avoid being petty (if you think you are) because that's just a no-no in all relationships, especially marriages.

Tip 7. Prioritize the happiness of your spouse and let them know often enough that you care about them even when you're busy with all your work. You can schedule a vacation or maybe go for a quick date to allow both of you to catch up and forget the hustle and bustle of life for a while. You should focus on each other rather than on needless things. One more thing I would like to add is that you should be more united in matters concerning finance because most of the time, each of you would have a different opinion on what 'spending too much or too little' means. So **pro tip:** always seek your spouse's opinion before making any large purchase. This way they will feel more involved and will let you know their thoughts as well.

Tip 8. Learn to grow by focusing on each other's strengths and support each other's flaws and weaknesses. It might seem hard initially. However, once you get the hang of it, it will become a habit you can't break. Additionally, I would suggest going to bed together so that you can crunch in the time to snuggle, share how your day went, and discuss any possible problems.

Top 9. If you have a goal, share it with your spouse and seek their thoughts and opinions. If they have a goal or a plan, then support them and reach the goal together. Cheer for them and motivate them to fulfill their dreams. A true partner always encourages the dreams of their spouse no matter how big or small they are.

Tip 10. Instead of doing something that you don't like, why don't you try doing something that you both enjoy? It's important to say 'No' to your spouse sometimes and let them know why you don't want to perform a specific task or activity. Avoid compromising too much either because then you would deprive yourself of your joy and no one wants such resentment to jeopardize their marriage, right? So, search for opportunities that allow both of you to enjoy every activity and make them memorable.

Oftentimes, things like stress, problems, and responsibilities may get in the way. But if you believe in your relationship, then you'll always come out stronger and closer regardless of the obstacles you face. Learn to respect each other's decisions and always express your gratitude towards them. It's these little things that make up a marriage or a relationship. It may not all be a bed of roses, but marriage is something that you should undoubtedly experience and protect.

Don't let anyone tell you what or what not to do in your relationship. Just focus on the positive aspects and be each other's armor. Once both of you communicate well, you can fight any battle that may come your way.

Marriage doesn't just work one way. Both spouses must work hard to achieve the same goal which is togetherness regardless of what each individual is going through. There are four significant factors that make a marriage successful.

Commitment. Honesty. Respect. Love.

Commitment is not an option. It's a choice. So, whether you wish to commit your life to your spouse or not, it totally depends on you. Being committed to one another shows how much you love each other and how you would go through any problems together without blaming each other. Commitment requires effort. However, if you're willing to do it, then you're one of the most amazing spouses ever and your partner is lucky to have you.

What prevents a relationship from blooming and flourishing into something beautiful is when you are not honest enough with yourself and your spouse. Just as honesty leads to great things, honesty in relationships can play a huge role in keeping you and your spouse on the straight path and by each other's side always. Once trust is broken, it becomes harder for either spouse to commit to the other or be themselves around their spouse.

As for love and respect, they go hand in hand. If you don't love your partner, then you most likely wouldn't respect their decisions. That is why to love your spouse is to respect their decisions on all their concerns, no matter how big or small.

If you have these factors and you follow the book of God, you're sure to find success in marriage and have an unbreakable bond with your partner.

CHAPTER 16

PROBLEMS IN MARRIAGE

"Above all, love each other deeply, because love covers over a multitude of sins." –

~1 Peter 4:8 {NIV}

Marriage isn't always happily ever after. There will be times when you and your spouse will face differences. It may be in opinions or foreign affairs. In this chapter, I'm going to list some of the common problems that can happen in a marriage and how you can tackle them.

Problem #1 – Infidelity

Infidelity is when one spouse cheats on the other. It's a common problem that takes place in most marriages. Infidelities can be of many types, such as one-night stands, relationships on the internet, physical intimacy, or full-blown affairs.

"Marriage is honorable in all, and the bed undefiled: but whoremongers and adulterers God will judge". Hebrew 13:4 {KJV}

You can repair this lost (or should I say awkward) connection by forgiving each other and reconnecting in a way that will help both of you build back your trust. The spouse who's cheating must leave all affairs behind and prove to their partner that they will never cheat again. We all make mistakes but the one who forgives and forgets is held in higher regard and their reward will be with the Lord.

Problem #2 - Values/Beliefs

Although you may have discussed your core values and beliefs during your courtship, may take several arguments and fights for both of you to get used to them. Try to sit down and talk it out with each other. Recall what both of you discussed and work on them accordingly. Solve this problem quickly before you plan on having kids because if you fail to, there might be a dispute in regards to the values and beliefs your child or children will grow up with.

Problem #3 – Stress

We all go through stress regardless of our age. Even kids these days get stressed about whether they will get more likes on Instagram and Facebook and teenagers get stressed whether they will enter their preferred university or not. Life is all about stress but if you're prayerful, the stress will feel just like dandelions flying away in the wind.

Although it seems easy for me to say all these kinds of stuff, stress is another common problem in marriage that could jeopardize the relationship between you and your spouse. Stress can be triggered by various factors such as finance, family issues, or even mental and health issues. There is a tendency for you to blame your partner for your stress. This isn't good and it is outright unhealthy.

You can manage your stress by following a daily routine and habit together with your spouse and by seeking professional help. If your partner feels that you are stressed for some reason, you must accept the fact that you weren't open enough with them and you should confide in them. Let them know what you're going through or ask them what they're going through. You can even write down your thoughts in a diary/journal and after a while, read what you have written so that you can get to the roots of your problem.

Stress is temporary while your relationship is permanent. So, strive hard to be happy and healthy with them because the last thing you want is to lose your partner just because both of you weren't on the right terms.

Problem #4 – Boredom

Every relationship needs that kick as often as possible and if your relationship feels dry and unromantic, then it's high time you watched more romance movies and implement what you've watched because your love life needs to be saved. Boredom can occur when you, your spouse, or both of you are doing the same thing every single day without change. Things will definitely get boring. It's time to switch things up a bit and perhaps make things a lot more interesting.

You could decide to take a leave from your work and go on a wild vacation or relive your honeymoon. If you're a child at heart, you could go to amusement parks or aquariums and just break the repetitive cycle that has held you both back for so long. The list is almost endless. Trust me, even the slightest change in your routine will do the magic.

Problem #5 - Jealousy

Jealousy is 'okay' to some extent because it shows how much you love your spouse. However, when jealousy gets the better of you, it's going to be a problem for you and your spouse. You will always be jealous no matter who your spouse talks to, whether it's on the phone or in public.

Jealousy can take the life out of your relationship if you don't pull the reins on it back. You need to keep your jealousy in check. Learn to compromise a little as it's inevitable for both genders to get mixed while at work. And always communicate with your partner once you understand that you're the jealous type.

Some other problems include **lack of attention** and **appreciation, lack of communication, selfish behavior, anger issues**, and **lying**. Nevertheless, all of these can be solved if you have a strong mindset to make your relationship work better. Marriage is like a golden egg. It should be treasured and dealt with delicately. One little push and it might break. Child, hold onto that golden egg securely.

CHAPTER 17

MARRIAGE AS A WAY OF LIFE

"My command is this: Love each other as I have loved you"

~John 15:12 {NIV}

This is the right time for more emphasis upon Christian virtues in our marriage guidance, David Sanderlin addresses this in "The Christian Way to Be Happily Married." "We do not need to retreat to a monastery, convent, or mountain cabin for prayer, fasting, and a traditional contemplative life to become increasingly virtuous, Christ-like persons," says Sanderlin. He adds: "We can become increasingly virtuous, Christ-like persons in our own home by acting with love, wisdom and other Christian virtues in our busy marriage and family life."

Do you want to know the secrets required to create the kind of marriage and family relationships you want? This is the key: if you wish to marry in the way it has been intended to be, you need a vital relationship with the God who has created you and has the power to grant you a life of happiness and purpose. Psalm 16:11 tells us that there is "fullness of joy" is in the presence of God. Jesus Christ said, "I came that they might have life, and have it abundantly." He gives us a biblical plan for the functioning of family connections—and provides us with the power to pursue that plan through a relationship with him. He gives us a biblical plan for a successful and happy marriage.

In essence, marriage is an image of redemption that cannot be experienced any other way on this earth. We can obtain an accurate measure of

God's love for us only through our marriages. On the other hand, divorce makes a mockery of this image. God plans that you would remain married, even during the worst of times. As God keeps His vows and promises, He expects the same amount of devotion from you too. You will gain insights into God that will drive your faith and relationship with Him beyond your wildest imaginations by gaining such an understanding of the Christian philosophy of marriage. Indeed, through marriage, you can achieve an unparalleled partnership in joy, intent, and fulfilment.

CONCLUSION

"Be completely humble and gentle; be patient, bearing with one another in love, make every effort to keep the unity of the spirit through the bond of peace"

~Ephesians 4:2-3 {NIV}

Let the Bible instruct and guide your home. You shouldn't leave the Holy Spirit out of the place of your decisions as a family. There is sweetness in togetherness, and it will be sweeter if the couple is under the same headship, which is Christ.

In marriage, there will be certain times where your activities will become a routine. It is an everyday life that you have begun to live. Keep the fire of love burning. Don't get tired of loving each other. Instead, find reasons to love more. Be accountable to yourself and always try to agree with your partner.

Communication also matters a lot. Communication should foster a better understanding of each other. Exhibit your godly virtues and enjoy the blissfulness in your home.

"And over all these virtues put on love, which binds them all together in perfect unity". Colossians 3:14 {NIV}

Many people say that the hardest period of a marriage is year 5 -year 7 when you're most likely to divorce because of various reasons such as not being passionate about intimacy, not being satisfied as a parent, stress, depression, and increased responsibilities.

However, no marriage is stress-free, and no marriage is going to be perfect. You and your partner must work together to improve your relationship so that you can live happily in the long run. Adjustments and commitments must be made but that will be a simple process if you truly love them.

You can avoid some of the common mistakes people make years after getting married to ensure that your marriage remains in place.

1. Give your spouse a second chance. We all deserve second chances. So regardless of what may have taken place, forgive, forget, and give your partner another chance to prove themselves worthy of your love.

2. Talk to your partner even if it's about random or silly things. Crack jokes with them. Consider them your best friend and enjoy every single day as if it's your last.

3. Listen to your partner if you're ever in a fight.

4. Avoid any financial arguments and talk things through.

There are no hardest or best years of marriage. It all depends on how you take care of your partner and how much you both understand each other. Don't let any other articles overwhelm you. Just be yourself and believe in your spouse. Some marriages last forever and I hope your marriage is one of them.

Love is always in the air—at least that's what I think. We just have to inhale it and wait for the right moment where we will meet our knight/Dame in shining armor. This book which I have written will, hopefully, give you a clear insight on relationships as well as tips on how you can make it work.

Nowadays, people just want to have a quick relationship like they're getting a burger from a fast-food restaurant. But that's not how a relationship works. A fling or speed dating doesn't count, but a true relationship is when a couple looks at each other, feel each other's voice, sense each other's emotions, and empathize with each other's stories. I didn't write this book for those who wish to be single for the rest of their lives, but for those who hope to pursue happiness through their partners.

Now, after reading this book, what I need you to do is to close your eyes for a moment and ask yourself, 'am I ready to be in a relationship?' If yes, then hurray to you but if no, ask yourself again, 'what's stopping me?' and work on those problems first. It's better to have a clear vision of what you want and when you want it before you get serious with another person.

You will find numerous articles that talk about relationships but trust me, this book has covered every little aspect of it so that you won't have to go anywhere else.

Join the conversation! I'd love to connect with you. Share your thoughts and comments about what you've learnt with me on social media. Be sure to follow on Instagram @LouisEtu, Twitter @LouisEtu, Facebook (Louis Etu), on my YouTube channel: Louis Etu, or by visiting my website at louisetu.com .

www.ingramcontent.com/pod-product-compliance
Lightning Source LLC
LaVergne TN
LVHW051844080426
835512LV00018B/3062